ISBN 978-1-333-61276-4
PIBN 10526050

This book is a reproduction of an important historical work. Forgotten Books uses
state-of-the-art technology to digitally reconstruct the work, preserving the original format
whilst repairing imperfections present in the aged copy. In rare cases, an imperfection in
the original, such as a blemish or missing page, may be replicated in our edition. We do,
however, repair the vast majority of imperfections successfully; any imperfections that
remain are intentionally left to preserve the state of such historical works.

MARGARET MAHANEY

Talks About Turkeys

Price, $1.00

INTRODUCTION
By Philip R. Park

MORE than a century and a quarter ago there was fired in Concord, Mass., a shot that was heard around the world. This shot terminated the domination of monopoly and marked the opening of a new era,—the building of a new empire.

Not less important to all lovers of turkeys is the shot fired in this same beautiful old town by Margaret Mahaney, when she first put an end to the bogy that has been hovering over the Turkey industry so long, i. e., *Blackhead*. Not less triumphant has been her conquest of practically all the ailments besetting this beautiful bird.

It is really beyond belief that Miss Mahaney has raised in a season 300 turkeys with a loss of less than 2 per cent, when for years the Experiment Stations and Agricultural Colleges, as well as nearly all poultrymen, have claimed that turkeys could not be raised in this State. All would recognize this as wonderful work if applied to chickens, but when accomplished with turkeys it is doubly wonderful. These same Experiment Station directors had told Miss Mahaney that she could not do the things she was already accomplishing, but when they visited her farm they held up their hands and departed, acknowledging that here was a woman who had performed the miracle.

Miss Mahaney was a wonderfully capable trained nurse who broke down at her work and was ordered to the country to save her life, urged particu-

MISS MAHANEY'S $150.00 PRIZE TOM

larly to take up some out-of-door work. Poultry keeping appealed to her from the first, but turkeys particularly for the reason of the difficulties to be surmounted. If she could do what others could not she would be satisfied. Anyone could raise chickens, but hardly anyone could raise turkeys. Here was a task that delighted her and a problem that appealed to her. The difficulties she encountered would have discouraged any one but a pioneer of her character. Her deep maternal instinct (and she is, figuratively speaking, mother to everything and everybody upon the beautiful estate where she lives) brought the babies and old turkeys through their blackhead troubles, and from her medical training, together with the aid she received from contact with members of her family who were physicians, she recognized symptoms and remedies which one could acknowledge as miracles and not overstep the truth. She has applied the fruits of her life work to the solving of a problem, and some day the country at large from Maine to California will raise its hat to Margaret Mahaney, the lady from Concord, Mass., who restored what was supposed to be lost:—the art of raising turkeys, —and that in confinement in poultry houses under practically the same conditions as chickens.

If you find time to go to Concord, by all means call on Miss Mahaney and she will make you welcome. She will show you more turkeys than have ever before been raised in one flock in the eastern states, and she will delight in telling you the simple methods she uses. On the following pages she will tell you in her own way how she accomplishes it.

We repeat, Miss Mahaney is a wonderful woman. She has a beautiful estate on which to produce these birds, but others are doing just as wonderful work with them by following her teachings.

TABLE OF CONTENTS

FULL-PAGE ILLUSTRATIONS

A LETTER TO MY READERS

A LETTER TO MY READERS

Turkey Park,

Concord, Mass.

My dear Readers:—

The following is a copy of a letter recently received by me, and which represents the type of communications I have received daily for over three years from all parts of the country:

My dear Miss Mahaney:—

Altho we are strangers to each other, I am writing you today, regarding turkey raising. I read some time ago in the "Boston Post" that you had good success in raising turkeys, so I take the liberty of writing you for instructions, if you will kindly give them to me. I have tried for several years to raise a few, but it has been a hard job. They would do well for about six or seven weeks, then grow sick with liver and bowel trouble and fade away. Now what is the trouble? What must they be fed with? Must they range or be kept in a yard? In fact, what way must I manage to raise turkeys? What is your experience? Please write me.

Sincerely,

etc.

It is in answer to such letters as the foregoing that I am placing my methods in book form on the market, in order to enlighten the breeders of turkeys and to inform them how I first succeeded where others have failed.

In the first place, I visited two or three farms in the country. I found that no care whatever was taken of the turkeys. A common hen was fairly well looked after, fed and kept warm. The turkey was supposed to forage for itself, roost on old wagons or any sort of roost that the bird found convenient at night and in all kinds of weather. Conditions were anything but sanitary. Inbreeding was permitted year after year, as one tom was thought sufficient for the hen turkeys of five or six neighbors.

I visited one farm in particular, which had on it turkeys from very nice stock, about twenty in all. Of course they were small and pale, and had not developed as they should have. They roosted in a sort of shed right off the barn cellar, so that they had access to the barn cellar, and they roamed around on the manure pile all day. The manure was turned down through an opening under the cows. The roof of that shed had no shingles on it, and in wet weather the rain simply poured down on those birds. It is only natural that conditions such as these will bring on roup and all kinds of diseases. The birds will not be developed and cannot possibly be strong enough when the spring comes to fulfill the duties of the breeding season.

Birds hatched amid such surroundings are tainted with roup and other afflictions.

It is not very long ago since I had a talk with a gentleman from Vermont. He told me that at one time Vermont made a large amount of money in turkey raising. When the turkeys got to be four or five weeks old, the raisers simply turned them out, and let them take care of themselves. Those that lived through the summer, weathered storms and all other sorts of hardships, they rounded up in the fall, fattened for market or sold for breeders. This was what they called "clear profit." Everyone can readily understand to what that "clear profit" has led.

The result is that our splendid bronze turkeys are dying out by the thousands each year, and within seven or eight more years, if something is not done to strengthen the turkey and keep it up to the standard of at least the common hen, our famous turkey of America will be a thing of the past. Whereas, if the turkey when hatched is given good feed as described in another part of my book, taken care of until the red is thrown, and then turned into a good, warm shed at night, kept dry and warm in damp weather, and fed reasonably, three-thirds of the trouble in raising turkeys can be avoided.

Care must be given to the breeding hens. They must be kept in sanitary quarters, given plenty of good feed, with four drops of tincture of iron to a gallon of water, plenty of lime and sand, about half and half, and left where they can eat it at their own convenience. If you give ground bone, have it very fine, for it is apt to lodge in the corner of the mouth and sometimes will cause ulceration. When this happens, the jowl of the bird will become swollen, and on close examination, there will be found a small piece of white bone which will have to be removed and the mouth washed with Sulpho-Napthol or Presto Disinfectant. I generally use my salve two or three times before the wound is healed. If the bird that lays the eggs is good and strong, the turkeys that are hatched will be strong and rugged, and to *"keep them growing from the start"* has always been my motto.

In my closing paragraph I wish to say to all my readers that I have been most sincere and straightforward in everything that I have written in this book. To one and all who may read this, I extend a cordial invitation to visit my turkey farm in Concord, Massachusetts, that you may see for yourselves the progress I have made in the last eight years in raising turkeys in yards under the same conditions as chickens, a feat which has been claimed heretofore by experiment stations to be impossible to accomplish, in poultry-congested New England.

I have labored with the problem of turkey raising for many years, and sincerely believe myself to be in a position to advise others who may be beginners, as I once was, concerning the difficulties of turkey raising, and the best method of overcoming them.

I remain,

Sincerely yours,

MARGARET MAHANEY.

March 19, 1913.

FACTS ABOUT TURKEY RAISING

FACTS ABOUT TURKEY RAISING

THE one great essential on the part of a person raising or attempting to raise turkeys is patience, or persistency, whichever you care to call it. To anyone thinking of starting in this work I can only say that you will meet with plenty of difficulties and much that will discourage and dishearten you, but when you remember that each failure or discouragement means just that much more added to your knowledge of, and experience in this work, it should give you heart to keep on, and if you do keep on and on, using each little bit of experience thus gained and using it to good effect, in the end success is bound to come. I am going to tell you a few of the discouraging things that happened to me, and also of my method of raising turkeys, a method based on long experience and perfected in the face of many discouragements, and I hope that in the telling, you may learn something that will be of benefit.

I started with twelve turkey eggs. Had I known then how hard they are to raise, I wonder if I would have attempted it? I hatched out eight turkeys from that lot of eggs, and I raised just one. I named her Hen-Hen, and she is on my place today, and is at the head of all my flock.

The following year I hatched out over thirty turkeys, and only succeeded in raising four. My work was then carried on on low land. The next year, I put old Hen-Hen on higher ground, where I am raising all my flock today.

She hatched out fifteen turkeys, and I raised all but one. I killed off some of the young toms, and kept all the pullets, all of which I still have, and they are splendid, strong stock, short-legged, heavy and a splendid bronze.

I then sent to Kentucky and brought out some of the best stock I could find down there, and then began my battle to raise turkeys. I had very good success, that is, as far as I went. At first, I knew hardly anything about the proper way to feed, and the right food to give my turkeys, but as the years went by, my experience in feeding taught me a great deal.

BREEDING

Now I will tell you in as concise a way as possible, the method I consider proper in raising turkeys. In the first place, it is necessary to have a good, strong two-year-old hen to breed from with a tom that is no relation whatever to the family. One of the foremost things you must be particular *not* to do is to inbreed. I much prefer a common hen to put my first hatch of eggs under; that will give the turkey hens a much longer time to lay. I consider it better to put my *turkey* hens on my June eggs. I put fifteen eggs under a turkey hen, and twelve under a common hen.

When the little turkeys come out, I disinfect their heads and under the wings with my own salve. Have you ever seen a little turkey that has a cold in its head wipe its beak under its wing? I have many times found the feathers under their wings matted as a result of this ill-bred habit of theirs. That, of course, is not a healthy state for a young bird that is

SHOWING STYLE OF RUNS

growing, and that is the reason that I disinfect with my salve under their wings and on their heads, and they always seem brighter afterward.

I have good, strong runs, 5 feet long and 4 feet wide, with high coops and thorough ventilation from the top, which carries off all the impure and overheated air, and keeps the temperature normal at the bottom of the coops for the little turkeys. On hot days I cover my runs with burlap.

The turkeys must be kept clean and dry and their straw must be well aired every day. Once a week, I wash out the bottom of the coop with disinfectant, and put in clean straw.

I give them all the lettuce they can eat three times daily, as the secret of raising turkeys is to keep their bowels in good order, and the droppings a bright green. Just as soon as I see a little turkey with its wings drooping, I take it away from the others and treat it as described on page 82.

I have invented my own pills for the cure of blackhead and they are now being largely used by turkey raisers all through New England.*

When my little turkeys are about three or four days old, I give them *Margaret Mahaney* Turkey Feed, and a little skimmed milk with a good solid feed of lettuce—all they can eat. At noon, I feed them lettuce again and clean water containing tincture of iron, 4 drops to each gallon of water. At night, I feed them bread soaked in milk and lettuce cut up fine with an onion and a shake of red pepper. After

*The call has been so heavy that it has been impossible for me to handle the business of the remedies from my Concord home, and they are now for sale with The Park & Pollard Company of Boston.

having dry feed all day, they relish the soft feed at night. There is no reason why, if you use my method in raising turkeys, and have your runs on high ground, you cannot be successful.

If the turkeys are raised in the right way, they are no harder to raise than chickens. When the pullets are about four months old, they should be given Epsom salts twice a week (a small teaspoonful to a gallon of water). This keeps the turkey in good condition and the blood cool. Also a tablespoonful of sulphate of iron in a pail of water should be left in some place where they can drink it. Keep them good and dry until they are ready for shipment, for turkeys are subject to blackhead until they are one year old.

I will be only too glad to give any information in my power to people who are interested in this subject. While the Experimental Colleges have put out some bulletins on the care of turkeys, the person that is going to issue a report on the raising of turkeys must get out in the field and be with them from the time they are baby chicks until they are ready to be disposed of, and then it will be many years before he will know all there is to know about turkey raising. I have spent years on my turkeys, and I think that I am now in a position to give any information that any grower may require in regard to this matter.

BRIEF OUTLINE OF MY METHOD
OF RAISING TURKEYS

THE MAHANEY SYSTEM DEVELOPS STRONG, HARDY BIRDS

BRIEF OUTLINE OF MY METHOD OF RAISING TURKEYS

IN the first place I select a good quiet hen that has been setting two or three days and put her in a deep, warm nest, not too far from the top of the box, so that when she goes to feed, the hen will not break the eggs by jumping on them when she returns to the nest. Twelve eggs seems a great number of turkey eggs to put under one hen, but that is what I put under every common hen, and I sometimes hatch out all the eggs. I spray the nests well with sulphur and also use my salve on the hen up until the sixteenth day. I never put any disinfectant on the hen or on her nest after that because there is life inside the eggs by that time, and the disinfectant is very apt to kill it.

When the eggs begin to hatch, some will hatch out before the rest; these I take away, placing them in a good warm box wrapped in flannel and keep them good and warm until all the eggs are hatched out and the mother able to receive them. When they are two days old, I put the young turkeys in a good clean coop, well whitewashed and waterproof. My runs are 5 ft. long and 4 ft. wide. I shut my little birds up in the coop for the first four days, until they become good and strong. After that, if the weather is fine and warm, I let them out about ten o'clock and put them in about three o'clock.

Their first food consists of a hard boiled egg, a shake of red pepper and three parts dandelion, cut up fine. You can give them all the green food they will eat, and also powdered charcoal and fine grit. After they are 3 or 4 days old, I give them bread and milk squeezed dry, and the *Margaret Mahaney* Turkey Feed.

The young poults are kept in runs which should be moved to a new spot each day and care taken that they are kept clean, dry and warm, and the straw must be taken out of the coops and thoroughly aired and kept good and clean, as the sanitary condition is half the battle in raising turkeys. Place your runs on a side hill, facing the south. On hot days, cover the runs with burlap.

Let them out into the runs for two hours or more every afternoon that is pleasant and dry until the time the birds are nine weeks old. Do not let them out in damp weather before they are two years old, for they are very susceptible to dampness and should be kept housed and warm in rainy and damp weather. While the little birds are out, watch carefully for hawks and pests.

Give the turkeys all the milk you can afford to give, as this will keep them growing. Plant a good field of lettuce and give them all this vegetable they can eat, and you will find that they will eat lettuce three times a day with good relish.

One of the secrets of raising turkeys is to keep the droppings a bright green; that, of course, keeps the liver in good condition, and goes a long way in keeping blackhead out of the flock. Take some lime, slack it, put half sand with it and make a sort of soft mush out of it. Place this on a board and dry it; then crumble it up and leave it around where your little turkeys can get it to eat.

"GIVE THE TURKEYS ALL THE MILK YOU CAN"

Keep them in dry, tight houses with the south side open so that they may have an abundance of fresh air without draughts.

When it is time to let them out of the runs, you can let them out for three and four hours at a time; you will find that they will want to go back to the runs when they become tired. Do not give them much feed at night; give them plenty of time to digest everything in their bowels, and they will then be ready for a good morning meal.

THROWING THE RED

When they show signs of throwing the red, put four drops of tincture of iron to a gallon of drinking water three or four times a week. If it is cold, rainy weather, put a drop of aconite in the water every day while the wet weather lasts. This will prevent their taking cold, and, as cold is the first sign of blackhead and diarrhea, it can be easily seen that a little precaution is worth more than a pound of cure.

In regard to keeping lice off the little turkeys—you must disinfect your hens and the turkeys very frequently. My salve for that purpose is a convenient and effective remedy.

If you will do as I have instructed you in the above paragraphs I do not think you will have much trouble in raising turkeys. Keep them dry by all means until they are five months old.

BREEDING

BREEDING

SELECTION AND TREATMENT OF BREEDING STOCK

THERE are some rules that must be followed in the selection of turkeys for breeding if it is hoped to succeed. Careless indifference has given no end of trouble to turkey raisers. In some instances which the writer has investigated all the turkeys owned in one locality have descended from the one original bird purchased many years before! In one case it was said that for twenty years no new blood had come into the neighborhood. If this foolish procedure had been continued it would have resulted in the destruction of the constitutional vigor of the turkeys.

A few plain rules which may be observed to advantage are as follows:

1.   Always use as breeders turkey hens over one year old.   Be sure that they are strong, healthy and vigorous, of good medium size.   In no instance select the smaller ones but do not strive to have them unusually large.

2.   The male may be a yearling or older.   Do not imagine that the large, overgrown males are the best. Strength, health and vigor with a well proportioned medium size are the main points of excellence.

3.   Avoid close breeding. New blood is of vital importance to turkeys.   Better send a thousand miles for a new male than risk the chance of inbreeding. Secure one in the fall so as to be assured of his healthy and vigorous constitution prior to the breeding season.

No matter what variety of turkey may be selected for keeping, they should, above all things, be strong, vigorous, healthy and well matured, but not akin. Better secure the females from one locality and the male from another to insure their non-relationship rather than run the risk of inbreeding. In all fowls it is well to remember that size is influenced largely by the female and color and finish by the male. Securing an over-large male to mate with small, weakly hens is not wise policy. A medium size male with a good size female of good constitutional vigor and mature age will do far better than the largest male bird with the smallest females.

The wise farmer always selects the very best corn or grain of all kinds for seeds. Equal care should be given the selection of the breeding stock in turkeys. The best raised on the farm should be reserved for producers and the fact should be kept in mind that turkey hens of the best quality after their second and third year make the best producers. Keep your best young hens with this in view. Undersized hens that lack constitutional vigor are not the kinds to select for successful turkey breeding. When you stop to consider that the male turkey is half of the entire flock in the matter of breeding, we may be led to greater care in the selection. None can be too good for the purpose. Constitutional vigor is of the first importance. Without this he can have no value whatever for the purpose intended. Plenty of bone, a full round breast and a long body are important. No matter of what stock or breeding the hen may be, the male should be selected from one of the standard varieties. If the hens are of the same standard variety the male of the same variety should be selected so as to maintain the stock in its purity. Well selected individuals of some one of the several standard varieties will give better results than can be secured by cross breeding, which has a tendency to bring to the surface the weak points of both sides of the cross. Proper crosses may improve the first issue but if followed up they rarely prove successful.

NUMBER OF FEMALES TO ONE MALE

The best rule for mating is to confine in yards, using eight or nine females to one male; some say twelve, but all I ever mate to one tom is eight females. The result of this number is that all my eggs prove fertile.

When they are yarded and from

eight to ten females are kept, it is better to have two toms and keep one shut up while the other is with the hens, changing them at least twice a week. When they run at large on a farm they will naturally divide into flocks. Under such conditions use one male to no more than six females.

CARE TO BE GIVEN BREEDING STOCK

March and April are the two months of the year that the breeding hen should have particular care. In the first place, I keep them warm and comfortable, with a box of sand where they can dust themselves every day. There is no bird that takes such pleasure in dusting herself as the turkey. She will roll on the sand for hours at a time in the sun, and this makes her happy and contented.

At this time I feed plenty of *Margaret Mahaney* Turkey Feed with Oyster Shells always within reach and a mixture of wheat, oats, barley, a very little cracked corn and beef scraps fed three or four times a week. Give plenty of drinking water and three or four times a week put a drop or two of tincture of iron to a gallon of drinking water. This keeps the bird healthy and strong. Take half lime and half sand, make a mush of it and spread it on a board to dry. When it is hard, place it in a box and leave it where your turkey hen can get it to eat at her own convenience. That helps to mature the eggs. She is very tender at this time. All through the laying season she must be kept warm and comfortable. It all goes towards making a successful season of turkey raising.

MATING

March is the proper time to mate up your pens of turkeys. I put one tom in a pen with eight hens. I watch my turkey hens very closely to see that they are not injured in any way by the spurs of the tom. If the turkey hen goes around with one wing down, you will know that she has been hurt, and if you take her up you will probably find that her side has been torn by the tom. Wash her carefully with a disinfectant, and if the wound needs a stitch it had better be taken as it will heal quicker.

FEEDING DURING BREEDING SEASON

In February and March do not feed your turkey hens too rich food or too many beef scraps or food of any kind that will force the hens to lay too early. You do not want any young chicks hatched out before the first of May or the last of April. When my turkey hens start to lay I feed a ground feed that is put up under my formula by The Park & Pollard Company of Boston, Mass., which they are putting out under the name of *Margaret Mahaney Turkey Feed*, and which can be procured of them all ready for feeding. Have plenty of beef scraps and oyster shells within easy reach. Twice a week put tincture of iron in the drinking water, four drops to a gallon of water; allow one gallon of water to each pen. The tincture of iron keeps the birds strong and in good condition, as a young turkey hen is very apt to weaken after her first litter of eggs is laid. Sometimes they die if not properly cared for.

Keep on hand within easy reach, constantly, a mixture of half sand and half lime made into a soft mush. When dry crumble up and leave it where your turkeys can get it to eat. They will eat this ravenously and it helps to harden the shells of the eggs.

NESTS AND NESTING

When the turkey hen is ready to lay she will start in first by looking in all the corners, for if she is yarded up, it is her nature to look for a dark and secluded spot in which to lay. I place to eight turkey hens four good dark nests. I make these by using packing cases with the cover on and the opening turned towards the wall of the house, allowing just enough room for the bird to enter. I put good, clean hay in the box. The turkey hen will be very happy when she finds that nobody can see her in her nest. It will make her very contented, and as we are now breeding turkeys in the domestic state, almost the same as the common hen, why not give them just the same care? You will find in the long run that you will raise many more turkeys if a turkey hen is properly housed and kept warm during the cold months of winter. The turkey hen begins to grow her eggs three months before she begins to lay, and as we all know that the turkey is a very cold bird, it is only natural that she should be kept warm. My houses are comfortable, tight and dry, but well ventilated from the south side.

When the turkey hen has laid about eighteen or nineteen eggs she will show signs of wanting to sit. Very quietly take her off the nest, remove her to another coop, give her a good range to run in with plenty of *Margaret Mahaney* Turkey Feed. In the meantime set the eggs under two good common hens. I find that Plymouth Rocks make good mothers. I put eleven or twelve eggs under a good Plymouth Rock hen, and make a good round nest in a half bushel box, stuffing the corners well so that the nest will stay in shape, as a good nest is half the hatching. In the meantime the turkey hen having had her run has forgotten all about sitting, and has started to laying again and I put her back in the mating pen. This process can be repeated three times during the season as a turkey hen will lay three litters in succession. I let my turkey hens sit on my June eggs and these hatch about the tenth or eleventh of July. These make good hardy birds for the coming cold weather. Disinfect the hen with *Margaret Mahaney* Salve, per directions, before setting on the eggs.

HATCHING

To go back to the hatching of the turkeys; the eggs that are right under

FIG. 1 REDS AND PLYMOUTH ROCKS MAKE EXCELLENT MOTHERS

the breast of the hen will hatch first. Sometimes I do not wait for them all to come out of the shell, taking them away, say four or five at a time, thus giving the outside eggs a chance to hatch. The eggs which I take away I put in an incubator which has previously been regulated to the right heat. When they are all hatched, I have my coop well whitewashed and about six inches of good clean straw on the bottom. I place my biddy in the coop and put the little turkeys all around her. Be very careful in giving them drink or water that the little turkeys do not get wet, for they often take cold in that way.

FIRST FEED

The first feed that I give them is common sting nettle, chopped fine, with a hard boiled egg and a little shake of red pepper. You will find that they will eat the green stuff ravenously, and this acts on the bowels as a regular physic.

When they are three days old I begin feeding them the prepared ground feed, —*Margaret Mahaney* Turkey Feed— with a little wheat bread soaked in milk, squeezed dry and mixed with the egg and nettle. As The Park & Pollard Company carry this ground feed it can be easily had there. I keep this always before them. In the morning I give them nothing but the *Margaret Mahaney* Turkey Feed with a good feed of lettuce. At night I give them the sting nettle again with bread soaked in milk and squeezed dry and a little chopped onion, if convenient. You will find that the birds you feed the sting nettle to will throw the red three weeks before the ones that do not have it fed to them.

When the little chicks first come out, before you put them in the coop, you must remember to disinfect with my salve on the head and under the wings; also give the foster mother the same treatment with the salve, for if there are vermin on the hen they will leave the hen and go to the little turkeys and unless cared for the little birds will sicken and die. If affected with lice the bodies will become very red and irritated. You will find the lice especially under the wings or in the fringe of the wings. When the feathers do not grow evenly on a little turkey (some growing long while others are short) you will know that the turkey has lice, and you should at once "get busy." One or two doses of my salve will make a marked improvement. I always disinfect the hen when I put her on the eggs, but never disinfect her after the fifteenth day for at that time there is life in the chick, and you are very apt to kill it, as they breathe through the air cells of the egg.

THE SETTING OF THE TURKEY HEN

In the wild state the hen seeks the most secluded and inaccessible spot where there is protection from birds and beasts of prey. Security against attack is the main thing instinct prompts her to look out for. A tangled thicket of briars, a sheltering ledge, a hollow stump, a clump of brush filled with decaying leaves suits her fancy. With little preparation she drops her eggs on the bare ground in these secluded places. Domestic turkeys are usually allowed a good deal of freedom in choosing their nests. I generally set them the same as I do the common hen.

BREEDING PENS

A half bushel basket is a comfortable nest for a turkey hen, and will give plenty of room for fifteen or eighteen eggs.

Turkeys require a good deal of attention while they are on the nests. They should be in one yard or building, or at least, not far distant from one another that it may take as little time as possible to make the frequent visits necessary to each. Give the eggs room and have the nest deep enough to prevent their rolling out of the nest. A turkey hen will lay from fifteen to thirty eggs at a litter, but she cannot always cover the whole lot. Very large old birds will cover twenty eggs; smaller birds will cover from fifteen to eighteen which is about the proper number to allow one bird to take care of.

If you have a dozen turkey hens in your flock,—which is about the right number for a good range,—it will not be difficult to set several birds at once, and this may be arranged by placing the nests containing artificial eggs within a few feet of each other. You can keep part of the hens upon their nests a few days until three or four are ready to sit. Then select eggs of as near equal age as possible and put them under the hens that are sitting persistently. If the hens close together are not set at the same time, there is danger when the first begins to hatch that her neighbor will hear the peep of the first chick and perhaps forsake her nest. If all the group of three or four nests are hatching at the same time, there is no trouble of this kind.

Before putting the eggs in the nest it is well to disinfect the hen with turkey salve under her wings. It will prevent vermin of any kind.

If any of the eggs get fouled with the yolk of a broken egg before or after setting, the shells should be carefully cleaned with warm water to secure their hatching. Two or three turkeys will sometimes lay in the same nest. This will do no harm in the early part of the season, but they should be separated before setting, allowing only one bird to a nest. This may be done by making nests nearby and putting porcelain eggs into each new nest. Turkeys are not liable to crowd onto an occupied nest when there is a vacant one nearby. The group of hens that sit together, and bring off their young at the same time, will naturally feed and ramble together, and this will save time in looking after them.

The turkey is a close sitter and will not leave her nest for several days at a time. Grain and water should be kept near the nest all the time. When the turkeys begin to hatch I take the little chicks out just the same as I do when under a common hen, and give the ones that are not hatched a chance to do so.

When they are all ready to go into the coop, I lift the hen very gently and carry her to the coop, generally putting the little turkeys into the coops first as the turkey hen is a very nervous bird and will scratch around and sometimes walk on the little birds.

That is why I like to have them good and strong before they go into the coop with the mother. The little fellows seem to understand that the mother should not step on them for they will crowd over towards the side of the coop out of her reach. She will soon get used to them and to being fed and will settle down to taking care of her babies in good shape, as the turkey hen is a

TURKEYS SHOULD BE TAMED

very devoted mother. She will watch out for those who feed her and take care of her little babies. They will run to meet me when they see me coming, that is, of course, if they are out in the field. I have had them come home themselves when I let them out for a ramble, and when I have gone to feed them the mother would be in the coop with all her little babies.

I give the same treatment to the turkey chicks that are brought up by their mother as I do when they are brought up by a common hen, only the common hen will leave them long before the turkey hen will think of forsaking her babies. I have gone into the turkey house when they were five or six months old and would find a young turkey pullet nestling close to her mother. You do not find this in any other domestic bird that I know of.

THE THROWING OF THE RED
AND YOUNG TURKEYS

THE THROWING OF THE RED AND YOUNG TURKEYS

AS there seems to be some difference of opinion about the "throwing of the red," first let me tell you what the throwing of the red means.

More or less blood must flow into the brain and head of the turkey when it shows so plainly through the skin. When a turkey is five weeks old or even four, it is time for it to begin to "throw the red," as when blood comes from the liver and heart, of course it must have some action on the little pullets. I have had young turkeys throw the red in five weeks, and show it very plainly, —that is after being fed twice a day on sting nettle. On the other hand, before

I knew what to feed to them, I have had them linger along up until seven or eight weeks, and at the end of that time, they would usually die. What had happened was that the blood had returned to the liver, become stagnant and caused diarrhea, which, of course, caused the death of the young turkey. When a young turkey is in good condition it ought to shoot the red from the beginning to the end in ten days. Of course it will not be as prominent as in a larger bird. As the bird grows, the red becomes more apparent.

When the little turkey is about four weeks old the feathers will begin to fall from the head some. Then you will know that the critical time is at hand. The little bird begins to shoot the red. It mopes around sometimes for days. There will be nothing wrong with him except that he just does not feel well.

Give plenty of sting nettle and a little tincture of iron three times a week (4 drops of tincture of iron to a gallon of drinking water) and you will see an improvement in a couple of days.

The young toms are much stronger than the pullets. Some of them will shoot the red and grow splendidly all through it with no signs of any drooping whatever, but there is always a marked change in the little pullets.

After the red is grown, the secret of success in turkeys is to keep them growing. You can give them all the skimmed milk and all the sour milk they will drink. Feed them all the lettuce they can eat three times a day with nettle in the feed, if you have it on the place. It is one of the necessities in raising turkeys that you keep the liver clean and if you feed lettuce two or three times a day, the droppings will be a bright green and in good condition.

For my birds I have large runs, 6 ft. each way, which makes a good square run. I move the runs every day to clean ground; the straw is taken out and aired. If it is damp weather, put clean straw in at least every other day. My coops are high and well ventilated at the top which takes off all the hot and impure air, and helps keep the little turkeys strong and healthy. I allow about ten runs out at a time consisting of ten birds each and let them go for a good long ramble. They do not stay away from their houses very long, however, but soon get tired and come back, usually staying out about two hours. Then I put them in their coops and let out about ten more runs. When I put them back into the coops I feed them lettuce and clean drinking water.

(I continue this process until I have let out the entire flock.) I let out so many runs at a time so there will be no confusion in putting them in. I do this daily, every fair day, until the turkey is four or five months old. Then I let them all out together. I put them in larger houses every night, keep them good and warm, with good roosts and clean straw, and I have very little trouble from disease.

Every turkey should be allowed out for a while each day if the weather is fine and there are no signs of rain. If it is lowery or dark, do not let them out until the weather is pleasant again. This method of letting them out keeps them growing rapidly and makes them very tame so that they can be handled much more easily.

Why not give a turkey the same care that we give a hen. People tell me many ways in which their turkeys are neglected. They seem to think that they do not need to look after turkeys and after they are hatched they turn them out and let them wander and forage for themselves. The time of that kind of treatment for turkeys is past. Remember we are raising turkeys now by the approved methods and full feeding applied to modern poultry raising. People will come to me and tell me that their turkey hens are roosting out in the trees nights when it is below zero. As I have stated before, if it is in January these turkey hens are beginning to grow eggs. What vitality is there back of eggs grown under conditions of that kind? None whatever.

On hot days you must cover the runs with burlap or shade of some description.   I use the burlap sacks in which I receive dried bread waste that I buy.

With reference to feeding bread, be sure never to feed bread that is mouldy for if you do you will start diarrhea in the young turkeys in no time.

When fall is coming on you must be very careful of the pullets.   As I said before, they are much more subject to blackhead than are the toms.   When I house them up,—that is, in large houses, say forty or fifty to one pen, I have my prepared feed for turkeys (*Margaret Mahaney Turkey Feed*) before the pullets all the time.   The less corn you give any turkey hen the less trouble you will have from blackhead, for corn is heating.   To keep the pullets in good condition you will find all the ingredients in this prepared feed, which is put up and sold now by The Park & Pollard Company, 46 Canal

Street, Boston, under the name of *Margaret Mahaney* Turkey Feed.

Give more or less whole corn to the toms if you want to get them in good condition for shipping or for dressing around Thanksgiving. They do not fatten up as quickly as the turkey hen, which is the reason I keep all corn and corn meal away from the turkey hens.

Put one-half teaspoonful of salicylate of soda in the drinking water in each pan at night. In the mornings give them fresh water and twice a week place in it a little tincture of iron (4 drops to each gallon of water). Do this up to about January, and then, if your turkey hens are kept warm and comfortable, they are over the dangers of the blackhead season.

Give the same treatment to the young toms.

INVESTIGATION OF DISEASES

"WHAT *is* the disease?" is the first and most important question to ask. The number of people who fatefully assume from the beginning that the answer to this question is beyond their reach is inexcusably large. If the non-professional reader would apply even a limited amount of study and common sense many of the lesser ills might be avoided, and many others successfully treated. A little special instruction is here given to enable one to detect a disease before it is too late, and thus, in a great measure, to avoid those disheartening ravages which, at times, come upon the uninformed owner of turkeys.

Page sixty-five

The small number of diseases which are liable to be confused makes it comparatively easy to form the right conclusion by eliminating from the possible list those that do not show the particular symptoms of the other diseases.

A general knowledge of the organism, habits, and appearance of turkeys when in health is, of course, very desirable. A reasonably close observation is about all we can expect in this matter from the ordinary owner of a large flock of turkeys. The experienced fancier adds to this a frequent handling and more detailed study to learn the normal hardness and suppleness of the flesh and the warmth, moisture and color of the skin, especially about the vent, and the outline and structure of the skeleton. It is also eminently desirable that one know what is a right condition of all the organs, but this is particularly true in respect to the liver and other digestive organs.

One of the most common mistakes in the discovery of a disease is the forming of a decision after too little study. Finding one or two symptoms which are known to attend a suspected ailment, one is prone to jump at the conclusion that he has detected the real difficulty, when a further investigation would reveal other symptoms, which, in conjunction with these, would lead to the true conclusion. Every examination, therefore, should be thorough until a degree of certainty is felt. It is essential, too, that the raiser not expect that the disease will invariably present just the symptoms mentioned in any book, for they will vary more or less in different turkeys, and even in the same one at different times,—a caution which merely calls for the exercise of judgment and common sense.

When any doubt is felt on the contagious nature of a disease, the affected turkey should be removed from the flock until the possible danger is passed. When a bird dies from an unknown cause, it should be opened and the condition of the internal organs noted, along with a study of their condition as taken up in the following pages of treatment.

In general, it may be observed that the presence of lice and mites is often the cause of weakness and loss of condition, especially if the turkeys are allowed to roost with the common hens.

BLACKHEAD

BLACKHEAD

A GREAT many people write to me, saying that they lose their pullets and young turkeys after they have grown the first feathers. I never lose a turkey at that time. I grow my turkeys in runs as you would chickens and it is a beautiful sight to see well onto three hundred healthy, strong turkeys in runs placed side by side. I never have any trouble with my young turkeys. As I said before in another part of my work, blackhead never appears in my flock until the turkey is six and seven months old. When I see any signs of blackhead, I move all my turkeys to new ground, disinfect all my coops with Presto Disinfectant, and start in to cure my blackhead, as described on page 79. I wait for a wet day, and put lime on the ground that I moved the coops from, as turkeys are very apt to return to their old dwelling place. In that way, I keep down blackhead. It is a very simple disease if taken in time and easily cured.

When I first started raising turkeys, my little pullets died after they were feathered and about seven or eight weeks old. Some of them would not shoot the red until they were weighing two and a half pounds. Their heads would be dark, and their steps slow and dragging. As I said before, the blood lay dormant in the liver, and thus started blackhead. If a turkey does not throw the red, when seven or eight weeks old, on close examination it will be found that the abdomen is dark and of a bluish cast. The flesh is not in good condition, whereas in a young healthy turkey that has thrown the red at that age, the flesh will be pure and white.

MY FIRST SUCCESSFUL FIGHT AGAINST BLACKHEAD

When I first started to raise turkeys, and one came down with blackhead, I thought that there was no cure for her. I did all I possibly could, and if she died, I judged that she had to and that there was absolutely nothing that could be done to prevent it.

One year I brought two handsome pullets in from Kentucky. They were fine, strong handsome birds, well marked, with splendid barrings, and a beautiful bronze. I grew extremely fond of them. When the spring of the year came on, about the last of March, around laying time, one of those two birds came down with blackhead and I determined that I would make a fight for her life.

She was an extremely sick bird. I took her into the house, placed her in the back hall, in a cast-off oval shaped clothes basket. I put soft burlap under her and wrapped her up warmly. I had a good knowledge of homeopathic remedies, and I started to cure bowel and liver troubles. The fever I kept down with aconite by giving a drop in a little water every hour. I stayed by the side of that turkey all night long. There were times when she would scream with pain, and then I placed her feet in water as hot as she could bear it with plenty of mustard in it, and allowed the water to come up as high as the first joint of her legs. I allowed her to stand in that about ten minutes at a time, and then I dried her feet and legs and placed her back in the basket. She would be very weak after this treatment, but seemed easier. At other times she would become weak and lifeless, and I would then take her up in my arms, go out-of-doors and let her have the benefit of the cool air. The fight went on in this way until four o'clock in the morning, when she opened her eyes, raised her head, looked up at me and chirped a little. I decided then and there that there was such a thing as curing blackhead.

I did not know then so much about the stoppage in the bowels. I did know, however, that nothing had passed through her bowels. I gave her a little warm whisky and milk, some more of my remedies, and then went for a couple of hours' rest myself. When I went to her again about two hours afterward, the red had begun to flow back into her head, the fever had left her, and her pulse was normal. The pulse of a turkey begins to beat just above the crop and in case of death, will gradually creep up until, just before the breath leaves the bird, it will have reached a point under the throat. I kept the pulse in this bird down to the middle of the neck; I never let it get any further. There were times when I had to place a cloth dipped in ice water on her head, but I was fighting for the life of my little pet, and she seemed to realize what I was doing. She was very weak all the morning. I took her up, placed her out on the lawn in the sun, and she staggered to her feet about twelve o'clock of that day, and then a solid core came from her bowels. This had lodged in the cecum. At that time I knew very little about this trait of the disease. Attached to the core was a part of the lining of the intestine. The turkey hen was very weak for days. One thing in

FRIENDS (MISS MAHANEY AND "GRANDMA CLEAVES")

her favor was that she had an empty crop, and I immediately fed her a tablespoonful of cold water in which was dissolved four grains of common alum. That was given in order to form a skin and harden the sore and raw place in the bowel after the bird had passed the core. The turkey hen did not fully recover for three or four days.

That turkey hen is about one of the best I have on my place. I call her Grandma Cleaves. The Agricultural colleges maintain that a bird that has once been afflicted with blackhead is unfit for breeding stock. I have in my possession a young tom that was hatched out the fifteenth day of July, 1912, by that bird. He weighs 31 lbs. and is well developed in every way. She laid three litters of eggs last summer, and sat on the last litter, hatched twelve turkeys and raised eleven in that flock. In my opinion, a bird that has passed through blackhead is one of the best and strongest birds to breed from. I never had a bird come down the second season with blackhead. It is just like any other common fever that is contagious, and can afflict a person but once.

After winning that fight, I made up my mind that something could be done for blackhead, and from that time on I have had great success in battling against this disease.

My breeding grounds are not so far distant but that the people of Massachusetts can come to see me. I would be very glad to show them my runs and turkeys and my methods of breeding.

TO DETECT BLACKHEAD

Blackhead is the disease to be most dreaded by the turkey raisers in New England and all over the country.

When you go into the turkey house in the morning, go directly to the droppings board and see if you find any yellow droppings. If you do, look carefully over your flock. It will not take you long to discover the bird that has blackhead. The head is an unhealthy dusky gray, and the bird will mope around, apparently wanting to eat and yet not doing so. Then you can decide that you have blackhead in your flock.

TREATMENT OF FULL GROWN TURKEYS

Take that bird away immediately; disinfect her head and under the wings with salve; massage the crop gently to see if it is full of undigested food. If it is, give a scant half teaspoonful of Epsom salts in a little water. In about an hour's time give a tablespoonful of olive oil and follow with a quarter of a teaspoonful salicylate of soda in two tablespoonfuls of warm water. After the crop is emptied put her in a box, say a good sized packing case, with plenty of straw, and cover with burlap. Give a teaspoonful of warm whisky and a tablespoonful of milk mixed together. This will keep up the vitality of the bird. A long necked milk testing bottle comes in very handy in a flock of any kind of fowl, for you can place the neck down below the windpipe and inject the liquids into the crop without any choking on the part of the fowl. Then watch and see if the droppings are yellow. If they are give one of the *Mahaney* Blackhead pills every hour until the droppings become normal. You can place the pill on the tongue of the turkey and make her swallow it. If there is nothing in the crop except a brash of sour wind, give the pills and hot milk and whiskey at once.

Be sure to keep the bird warm **for** a few days, and then disinfect before she goes out with the rest of the flock. Look over the droppings board every morning and see if there are any yellow droppings. Use plenty of lime. Twice a week, in the morning, give sulphate of iron, powdered (one level teaspoonful in a gallon of water in an earthen dish). The other days, at night, give salicylate of soda in the same amount in the drinking water. This will keep your flock in good condition.

BLACKHEAD IN YOUNG TURKEYS

The first symptom of blackhead in the young turkeys has the appearance of a common cold in the head. The turkey will sniff and water will sometimes come from the nose. The loss of appetite is apparent. The wings droop and when you let the turkeys out of the coops, the one affected will drag itself along behind the rest of the flock. I take that bird away from the rest. I disinfect the head and under the wings with my salve. Rub the salve lightly on the head. Hold the turkey gently across the back, press the wings down to the side. If you are not very gentle with them, and very careful, you are liable to break the wings.

The moment you see one become lifeless, with dragging steps and loss of appetite, disinfect the whole flock with the salve twice a week. Dissolve in an earthen dish four or five of the *Margaret Mahaney* Turkey Pills in a little warm water; then mix the solution in a quart of drinking water and give to the young turkeys to drink. This, repeated every day, with the straw well aired and kept clean, and the coop dry and water-proof, will make them show

MAKE THE MOST SUCCESSFUL TURKEY RAISERS

a marked improvement in three days. I never lose a young turkey. They thrive just as well as little chickens, and I think they are just as hardy.

As vermin is one of the enemies of young turkeys, use the salve twice a week always, and use it in the morning. Do not shut them up after putting on my salve because it is very strong. Let it evaporate before the little chickens go to bed at night, and you will have no vermin. There is an old saying about a louse in the head of a turkey which enters the brain and causes blackhead. I know very well that that does not cause blackhead, as this disease comes from a common cold, which descends to the bowels and liver and kills the turkey after a few days' suffering if not relieved.

Treatment of a Common Cold.

Blackhead starts from a common cold. When you have a bird in your flock afflicted with a cold, place a small teaspoonful of Epsom salts to one gallon of water. Do this three or four days in succession and put plenty of lime around your turkey houses. I put lime on the droppings boards every day; it will kill the disease in no time and do no injury to the turkey. Of course I put clean straw in my turkey house in damp weather every other day as the straw becomes damp and is very liable to breed disease.

Give this Epsom salts treatment in the hot weather whether the birds show symptoms of disease or not. It keeps their blood cool and avoids the tendency to disease.

The time for blackhead season is in

what is commonly called "dog days," that is, mid-summer. The weather is heavy and dark and is very injurious to young turkeys. That is the time you must keep your coops good and dry and give plenty of green stuff, with aconite in the drinking water about twice a week to keep down any fever. Three drops in a pint of water is all I give them as aconite is very poisonous. If you have any sting nettle at the time be sure to feed it, as sting nettle *is one of the greatest aids to success in raising young turkeys.*

When the turkey dies of blackhead the crop becomes apparently black and inflamed, and is very foul. The liver is enlarged, and has white or yellowish spots all over it. In some places it has the appearance of being eaten away. Underneath the liver, next to the back of the bird and around the heart you will find a brownish substance, just the same as you would find in a person who dies from peritonitis. You will also find in what is called the second stomach, that is, the bowel leading to the gizzard, a large core. Sometimes this will be very dark brownish yellow or ochre color, mingled with blood. This core forms a stoppage, and unless it is removed, is certain death for the turkey.

I have had turkeys die with what is commonly called in human beings, "appendicitis," as the appendix was matterated and badly swollen. In fact, in a bad case of blackhead all the bowels of the turkey become swollen. The gizzard is twice its natural size, the abdomen becomes swollen and black and the odor is very obnoxious. In a bad case of this kind there is nothing that can be done, the disease having become too far advanced, and that is why one ought to watch turkeys very closely. If the turkey is taken in time and *Margaret Mahaney* pills given, and the turkey is kept warm, (for they will take the disease first with a chill just the same as a human being would take malaria) there is no need of any loss in the flock from blackhead. All the colleges of agriculture have diagnosed the case as a parasite on the intestines, but I have thoroughly investigated that theory, and wish to say that I have found no grounds for such a belief.

COMMON DISEASES

COMMON DISEASES

RHEUMATISM

(Sometimes confused with Blackhead)

I HAVE a great many people write me in regard to weak legs in turkeys. Of course, this is common rheumatism. The limbs suffer an impairment or loss of use, are hot, swollen and stiff. The toes then being drawn out of shape, the fowl persistently sits down and cannot use the perch. The heart may become involved and this produces death. I had it in my flock one year,—that is, I had several birds victims to the disease. They would squat down all the time. The breast bone grew all over to one side from sitting so much. They were fat and apparently healthy, except that they could not seem to stand up any length of time. I bathed their feet with mustard and water as hot as I thought they could stand it. I saved most of them, but it seemed to me that they never could walk as well as the flock that had not been affected. The cause of this affliction is that the turkeys are allowed out too early in the morning when the dew is on the grass and allowed to roam around in damp places. At this time I was raising my flock on lowland. I have never had any of it in my flock since I moved to high and dry land. Give five drops of bryonia in a pint of drinking water to six turkeys. After using the mustard water be careful to wipe the turkey's legs dry and then rub well with camphorated oil the backs of the legs leading into the body. Keep in a warm and dry place and give sulphur in the feed (about a half teaspoonful to four turkeys).

TURKEYS THRIVE BEST ON HIGH LAND

"ROTTEN CROP" SOMETIMES MISTAKEN FOR BLACKHEAD

Another disease very common in turkeys which is called blackhead and yet has nothing to do with blackhead, is what you would call "rotten crop" in a common hen. When this takes place the crop becomes very foul and heavy. The bird will drink water, which stays in the crop and becomes sour. I have often had to take the bird up, hold the head down and rub the crop gently so that all the water would run from the mouth. With the aid of a long neck milk testing bottle I fill the crop with warm water with a quarter teaspoonful baking soda in it, and relieve the crop by massaging the second time. Then I give a tablespoonful of olive oil. Put the bird away from the rest, with very little feed for a couple of days. I never have any difficulty in saving a bird affected with what is commonly called "rotten crop." If not relieved, however, it will turn into blackhead and the turkey will die.

COLD—CATARRH—COUGH—BRONCHITIS

All of these are substantially different stages and symptoms of the same disorder. Exposure to wet and cold is the general cause. Cough is, indeed, a symptom, not a disease, and is connected with the other three. It may, however, attend other diseases, and when its cause is not known, the article pertaining to roup should especially be consulted. Bronchitis is but an advanced stage or aggravated form of cold or catarrh. The three are marked by more or less discharge from the eyes and nostrils, sneezing, wheezing, and, particularly in bronchitis, coughing and a rattling sound in the throat. To distinguish this from roup, see whether the discharge is offensive. If it is, roup is to be treated; if not, catarrh or bronchitis. In all cases of doubt, use the precautions detailed for roup.

Turkeys are subject to roup from the time they are babies, more so than common hens, as a cold is the cause of all their trouble.

Treatment: Remove the turkey to warm, dry shelter, and give warm, soft food. These measures will usually be sufficient, but the following will be valuable as aids: *For cold or catarrh* merely, and no distinction between them is here made, put three drops of strong tincture of aconite in a pint of the drink. If there is a swelling about the throat, two or three grains of the second trituration of mercuries three times a day will be useful. *For bronchitis*, in addition to the measures just named, give sweetened water for the drink, adding a few drops of nitric acid or sulphuric acid. *For both catarrh and bronchitis* give some stimulant, such as ginger or cayenne pepper in the food or whisky in the water. Treat catarrh and cold promptly, to keep them from developing into roup. Do not neglect bronchitis lest it run into consumption.

ROUP

Roup is a highly contagious malady which first affects the lining membrane of the beak and then extends to the eyes, throat, and whole head, eventually involving the entire constitution. According to its manifest symptoms, it has been called diphtheria, sore head, swelled eyes, hoarseness, bronchitis, canker, snuffles, influenza, sore throat, quinsy, blindness, and by other names. It attacks all ages, and will kill young turkeys in a very short time. Turkeys given poor shelter, and kept in filthy quarters, are subject to roup.

Symptoms: — Roup develops either slowly or rapidly, with the general signs of a bad cold in the head, such as wheezing, or sneezing, high fever and great thirst. The discharge from the eyes and nose is yellowish, being at first thin but growing thicker as the disease develops, and very offensive, closing the eyes, nostrils and throat (these parts and the whole head are swollen, sometimes enormously, so that blindness ensues, making the turkey unable to get its food, and thus hastening the decline of the system); pustular sores about the head and in the throat, discharging a frothy mucus; the breathing is impeded; the crop is often swollen; the comb and wattles may be pale or dark-colored. During the course of the disease the turkey is feeble and moping. A fatal case terminates in from three to eight days after the distinctive roup-symptoms set in, and those which are not treated when an epidemic is prevailing will generally be fatal. Upon opening a turkey that has died of roup one will find the liver and gall bladder full of pus, the flesh soft, of a bad odor, and, particularly about the lungs, slimy and spongy.

Treatment:—It is of the highest importance that the treatment begin as soon as the first symptoms appear. To detect the approach of the disease (and any turkey in the flock should be suspected if one has been infected), raise the wing and ascertain whether the feathers beneath it are stuck together, as the turkey has the habit of wiping its nose under the wings, and naturally the feathers will become matted and foul.

Remove the turkey to a good warm place; wash her head with warm water with a drop or two of sulpho-napthol in the water; dry well with a good soft cloth and rub *Mahaney* turkey salve on her head, throat and crop; open up her beak and oil the inside of her mouth and throat well with the salve. A little swab can be made for that purpose. Give one of the *Margaret Mahaney* blackhead pills, three times a day, and make a pill as large as a good sized bean as follows: one-half mustard and one-half sulphur, equal parts. Give the turkey one of these pills every night, and if swollen eyes and head has prevented her from seeing her food, feed her a little bread and milk, soft and warm, until she is able to feed herself. A drop or two of kerosene oil in the drinking water makes a good disinfectant for turkeys.

When a disease of this kind enters your turkey house disinfect your droppings boards, and feed five quarts of hot mash from *Margaret Mahaney* Turkey Feed with one or two onions chopped fine and put in the mash. A teaspoonful of red pepper also given to them every night before going to roost will help to prevent the disease from spreading. Keep your turkey house clean and dry, and if you see any sign of this disease, it is much better to remove the droppings every day, and if taken in time roup is not a fatal disease.

CONSUMPTION OF THE THROAT

The special symptoms of consumption of the throat are a frequent cough, roughness of the voice, and often a failure to partake of food either from loss of appetite or from pain caused by swallowing. Attacks of fever, followed by shivering, are more or less regular. For treatment keep the bird in a very warm atmosphere, chop up onions very fine and mix in the feed, also give a teaspoonful of olive oil three times a day with one to two drops of aconite to a cup of water.

I generally have what is commonly called a hospital for sick birds; that is, I set aside one coop, keep it warm and have it heated with an incubator lamp, a large one. The temperature should be kept around 70 degrees, until the bird ceases to cough.

CONSUMPTION OF THE LUNGS

A distinct feature of consumption of the chest or lungs is a tubercular deposit in the chest, liver and bowels. The first symptoms are a thinning of the voice and occasionally sneezing. When the sneezing comes on in the morning and continues during the day, the lungs have become involved, and eventually a puffed appearance will be manifest in the chest. Give the same treatment for consumption of the chest as given for consumption of the throat. Add a few drops of tincture of iron (four drops to a gallon of water) to the water each day until the appearance of the bird has improved.

Light, ventilation and pure air are three of nature's most potent agencies in counteracting disease. Every turkey should have a liberal allowance of sunlight, though the power and directness of the rays should be determined by the climate, which is only natural. Among those that need frequent sun baths are the wild birds of the air and as the turkey was originally a wild bird, in the very nature of things, it demands a great deal of sunlight. It makes no difference how hot the day is, the turkey will lie in the sun and seem to enjoy it when the temperature is even up to 100 degrees. This is the reason I keep my turkeys warm and comfortable, as it is a preventive of consumption or any disease of that nature.

A good dirt bath should be provided for a turkey all winter: light sand, half clay, with a measure of air-slacked lime. The turkey will wallow in that for an hour at a time, thoroughly enjoy it and seem so much brighter after it.

If turkeys are allowed to run on the frozen ground and roost in the trees all winter, how can one reasonably expect them to remain in a healthy condition when they positively need warm, comfortable quarters? If suitable houses are provided for turkeys, warm, clean and comfortable with plenty of lime, grit and charcoal during the winter months, it will be found that there will be very little trouble with blackhead during the summer and consequently less tendency to consumption and other diseases in the colder months.

SWOLLEN HEADS

Swollen heads in turkeys seems to me to be the prevailing disease this spring of 1913. Complaints have come to me from all over the country, also sick birds have been sent to me to treat.

I do not know whether it would be called roup or canker, but the appearance of it is that of a common cold, a watery discharge from the nose, eyes half closed, and sometimes wholly closed, with a large projecting formation in the orbital cavity under the eyes, which, if left there, will cause the death of the turkey after the turkey loses its sight. Press your hand gently on the formation. If the formation has not become hard, but is still in a spongy condition, press firmly on both sides of the nose under the eyes, and force out the thick, foul discharge which has gathered. Wash the head with Sulpho-Napthol or Presto Disinfectant, dry well, and then disinfect with my salve. Repeat this every day until the turkey is well. In the meantime the turkey will have a little hacking cough that is caused by a watery discharge from the head, which flows down inside the nose and drops on to the windpipe. A human being has a chance to relieve the head and throat, but the turkey does not have this advantage.

If, however, the formation in the orbital cavity has become hard, an operation is necessary. Have some one hold the bird gently on its side, with its wings close to the body in natural form, for in the struggle, the bird is very apt to break its wing. Wash the head with Sulpho-Napthol or Presto Disinfectant and dry well. Have ready a good sharp operating knife, thoroughly sterilized, and also sterilize your hands. About one-fourth inch below the eye you will find one or two leaders. You must try to avoid cutting through these. Always try to avoid cutting through any veins. Make a clean cut about one-half inch in length, running straight down the orbital cavity to the *beak* so that when it heals up it will leave no scar. If the turkey is in good blood and a male bird, they are very apt to bleed quite a little. I would then stop the blood with cotton batten, or by bathing with water mixed with a little alum. Leave the bird for that day. The next morning open up the cut, take out the canker, which you will find to be a yellow, cheesy substance, with a very bad odor. Remove all this canker, wash out the cavity with peroxide of hydrogen, dry well, fill the cavity with *Margaret Mahaney* Salve, which keeps the head soft and clean. Wash the head lightly for a few days. When the wound heals up you will find a sort of dry core in the wound. Remove this, wash out, and your turkey is all well. Trust the rest to nature.

If you find that the lump under the eye has become hard and white before you operate, and that the blood has flowed back from the head, there is no need of waiting for the wound to stop bleeding. You can remove the canker at once.*

In the meantime, in the feed put a half teaspoonful of sulphur each morning for a week in a warm mush made from *Margaret Mahaney* Turkey Feed. This will keep the bowels in good condition, and hasten the recovery of the turkey.

This canker is sometimes found in the rectum of the turkey. Syringe the bird with warm water in which has been dissolved a little piece of Castile soap. Add to one quart of water a half teaspoonful of boric acid, and after the bird has been thoroughly washed out, wash again with the above solu-

*For the operation above described I have been

using of late, and cannot recommend too highly, a knife which may be procured at Park & Pollard's, called a Killing Knife.

tion. Dry the vent thoroughly and sponge on a little sweet oil. Do this for a few days with sulphur in the feed, and you will find that the bird will be all right. Use about ½ teaspoonful of sulphur to ½ pint of feed.

SORE EYES AND HEAD

The eyes may become sore from dust, excessive heat, dampness and other causes, and give out a watery discharge. The whole head may become involved in the inflammation. Such mild afflictions are to be distinguished from canker and roup, but it is always safe to keep a sharp lookout for the latter when the eyes are sore.

Wash the parts with a weak solution of white vitriol (sulphate of zinc) or with alum-water, or with a solution of alum and camphor. If the discharge has become gummy or hardened, remove it with warm water and Castile soap, followed with alum and water. Dry the head well with a soft cloth, and then rub gently with *Margaret Mahaney* Turkey Salve, as it contains all the ingredients that heal and cleanse.

To about four turkeys put one-half teaspoonful of sulphur in the feed with a shake of red pepper three or four times a week, and a little tincture of iron in the water (about four drops to a gallon of water).

CONSTIPATION IN TURKEYS

Constipation is caused by indigestion, taking cold, too close confinement, too much dry feed and too little green, a deficient supply of good water and the like. It is indicated by frequent attempts to evacuate the bowels, either wholly unsuccessful or resulting only in hard, dark droppings. The turkey is uneasy and perhaps staggers.

Give an abundance of green food and a soft mixture of bran and oatmeal and ten drops of sulphate of magnesia to a pint of the drinking water. Along with these directions for the feed, it will be well to give two drops of aconite to a half glass of water, giving the bird a teaspoonful of the solution every hour until the fever disappears, following this with a solution made of two drops of nux vomica to a half glass of water, giving a teaspoonful of the solution every hour until well, or if a cold is the cause, use two drops of bryonia in the water instead of the nux vomica. I have often had this disease in my flock when the turkeys are about three months old, just before I let them out for a good day's ramble, so that is why I always recommend plenty of good lettuce. It keeps the bowels in good condition, keeps the intestines cool, and makes up itself for all fever remedies.

DIARRHEA.

This disease is often mistaken for blackhead in grown turkeys. It may result from an excessive use of tainted food, mouldy bread or mouldy grain, impure water, extreme heat, exposure in damp weather, filthy quarters and general indigestion, poison, or any inflammatory affliction of the intestines or the stomach.

The symptoms are loose droppings of different colors which befoul the feathers, lassitude, and a loss of condition. In dysentery which results from a diseased condition of the intestines, the droppings are more frothy and mingled with blood, and attended with rapid prostration.

A form of diarrhea essentially different from the two described, occurs in an old female turkey in which a white discharge comes away more or less constantly, often dribbling out, and keeps the feathers about the vent incrusted with a white, chalk-like deposit. It is doubtless due to some derangement in the shell-making function, and can best be treated by promoting the general health and using the means noted below.

Treatment: Have your pharmacist make up pills made of a mixture of five grains of powdered chalk, five of rhubarb, and five of cayenne pepper, adding a half grain of opium in severe cases. Give two pills daily. Another good remedy is camphorated spirits of barley meal, three to six grains for each bird according to age, or ten to twenty drops of the same may be put in a pint of the drink. For mild cases and in the early stages of others, powdered chalk on boiled rice may be sufficient. The remedy last named is recommended for the white discharge of old females, for which the pills described above should be used as well as a little lime water, made by allowing about ½ teaspoonful air-slacked lime to ½ pint water for a bird. Dissolve and then pour off the liquid for them to drink instead of plain water.

Restrict the drink in all forms of these disorders and put into it a little tincture of iron (four drops to a gallon of water).

Dysentery with blood discharges is a serious disorder. It is best to give a teaspoonful of castor oil, followed with three to six drops of laudanum every few hours, supplying an exclusive diet of mild food. It is important that the afflicted bird be kept quiet and apart from the flock, especially in dysentery.

Isolate the afflicted bird when you are at all doubtful regarding the nature of the disorder. Give a couple of table-spoonfuls of ground chalk to a pint of warm mash made from *Margaret Mahaney* Turkey Feed. This will also be found beneficial at any time to the laying turkey hens of five or six years old. Allow one pint of mash to four turkeys three times a day. A little camphor, about the size of a good sized bean, to four turkeys will hasten the recovery; dropped in the drinking water once a week, will help to keep the birds in good laying condition.

Diarrhea in Little Turkeys

Diarrhea in a little turkey is white, something the same as that trouble in a common chicken, and if you look very carefully you will see that the little legs are dotted with white, and the little turkeys will be lifeless and not appearing to thrive. That is the time to give them *Mahaney* pills (four to a quart of drinking water for 10 or 11 young turkeys). Boil a piece of meat, grind fine, and put in the feed, and that will help them get back their vitality. A drop of aconite in the drinking water on damp days will help to prevent fever of any kind.

GAPES

There are many remedies for gapes, but the following is always beneficial and dependable. It manifests itself first by the birds gaping around just as a person would yawn.

Fill a common, long-necked oil can such as is used for oiling a sewing machine, with kerosene oil; open the turkey's mouth and wait until it breathes in order that the windpipe may be open, then inject a good spray of the kerosene, perhaps a teaspoonful in all. Three doses will usually cure the turkeys of the gape worm. Give treatment three times a day, in the morning, at noon and night. Shut the turkeys up in their run for about a week, then move them to new ground.

TAPE WORM

The tape worm is an entirely different thing and is rather more serious, and will produce substantially the same symptoms as indigestion. If they are in the bowels, costiveness or diarrhea may be more marked, while the turkey will be uneasy and picking at the vent if they are in the lower part of the intestine. In all cases there will be more or less loss of flesh and often diminished gloss in the feathers, while the bird has either an impaired or a voracious appetite. The only unmistakable symptom is the presence of worms in the droppings when they first pass out.

An unhealthy condition of the digestive organs is the main cause. The treatment for this is a teaspoonful of castor oil followed by a light addition of sulphur to the feed, and this may expel the worms and restore the general health. A little cayenne pepper in the feed and tincture of iron in the water will aid the cure. The use of four drops of oil of ferm to a tablespoonful of water is beneficial in a case of this kind. Give in the morning before the bird has eaten anything.

I had one bird this last year which had a tape worm. I noticed the worm in the droppings first. I took the bird away and put her on a board floor and gave her a good dose of castor oil. She had only passed half of the worm at one time, and I watched her very closely until she passed the head.

In a case of tape worm the droppings will be more or less white and limy. A turkey requires a great deal of lime.

I have even seen turkeys pick at an old wall where it had been plastered. Lime, mixed with sand, should be left in all the corners of the farm for turkeys to eat, as it is a sure preventive of worms.

PERITONITIS

Peritonitis in turkeys is often mistaken for blackhead. It is a very difficult disease to treat, and it is only with the milder cases that success can reasonably be expected. The affected bird must be kept quiet, protected from any current of air, and opium in doses of one (1) grain every four hours is recommended to quiet the pain and reduce the movement of the intestines, or mix three or four drops of aconite in a half glass of water and give a teaspoonful three or four times a day. Injections of tepid water are recommended to counteract constipation. Take a hot water bag. Do not have the water so hot that it would be uncomfortable for the turkey; wring a flannel out of warm water and lay it over the hot water bag, and then place the bag against the wall of the abdomen. Renew them as often as necessary to keep up a moist heat. This treatment should be continued from a half hour to an hour. Repeat three or four times a day, drying the surface of the wall afterwards so that the bird will not take cold. If there is a great weakness, one or two drops of ether, or four or five drops of tincture of camphor may be injected under the skin as a stimulant.

In case the disease is due to rupture of the oviduct or perforation of the intestine, treatment is useless; if it has followed inflammation of the intestine, the treatment for enteritis should be combined with that for peritonitis.

On opening the abdominal cavity of a turkey which has died from peritonitis, the lining membrane is found to be a deep red in color, and is sometimes covered by an exudate, which may consist of a thin, transparent layer, or it may be thick yellowish or reddish yellow. The abdomen may contain more or less liquid which may be transparent or it may be turbid with a yellow or reddish color. If the trouble is due to the perforation of the intestine, the liquid will have a very offensive odor from the multiplication of the putrefactive germs. If it has resulted from the rupture of the oviduct, the egg, either intact or broken, will generally be found in the abdominal cavity, and the ruptured place in the wall of the oviduct is easily discovered.

The writer had two cases of peritonitis in her flock of turkey hens just around the laying season. One died and the other I succeeded in saving by the breaking of the bound egg and washing out the rectum with a syringe. For a wash of this kind four or five drops of iodine should be added. It is good to relieve pain and acts as a stimulant for the bird. The bird must be kept very warm and comfortable after a thing of that kind for three or four days. It is well to feed the bird on stimulating food and keep her away from the breeding pens until she recovers her strength.

THE BRONZE TURKEY

THE BRONZE TURKEY

THE ORGANS AND SIZE

THIS variety holds the place of honor. It probably originated from a cross between the wild and the tame product. Its beautiful, rich plumage and size have come from the wild progenitor. To maintain this quality, crosses are continually made. In this way the mammoth size has been gained. Their standard weight ranges from twenty, thirty-six to forty and fifty pounds, according to age and sex. Probably more of this variety are grown each year than all the others. They have been pushed on all sides, almost to the exclusion of the others. Until within a few years, if possible,

Missing Page

ing than the turkey. This should be guarded against at all times if it is hoped to gain the best results.

SELECTION OF BREEDING STOCK

Naturally the bronze turkey should be the largest in size, the most vigorous in constitution and the most profitable to grow. This would be the status of the variety at present were it not that too little attention has been given to the selection of the females for breeding stock. It should be fully understood that size and constitutional vigor come largely from the female, and to have this influence to the fullest extent, well proportioned, vigorous females in their second or third year should be selected as breeders. Do not select very large specimens for this purpose; those of a medium size are usually the best. Discard undersized females at all times, as they are of little value as producers. Length of shank and thigh, if out of proportion, should not be mistaken for size. Full rounded body and breast indicates value most clearly; size and strength of bone indicate constitutional vigor which should be maintained through the selection of the very best at all times for producing stock.

When especial care is given to the selection of breeding birds, and the grower bears in mind those profitable market characteristics — compactness of form, length of breast and body, and constitutional vigor, the most satisfactory results may be obtained from the growing of this variety, but no matter how much care may be given those conditions, only partial success will come if inbreeding is permitted. The use of over-sized males with small females is of less advantage than the use of smaller males with well matured, medium sized females.

MARKETING

Of course, we cannot all sell our turkeys for breeding. That would entirely rob the table of its Thanksgiving luxury. After the turkeys are grown and ready for market, quite as much care and attention should be given to the killing and shipping as to the proper growing. When these things cannot be done to good advantage, it would be better to sell them alive. Buyers who are prepared to kill, dress, pack and ship turkeys and to save the feathers, should be in a position to pay what they are worth alive, and should be able to handle them at a profit better than can the grower, who may not be prepared to do this work to advantage. So much depends upon marketing them in the best condition that small growers should either dress and sell to their home market or, providing it can be done at a fair price, sell alive to someone who makes a business of handling such stock. Kill nothing but well fattened stock. It seldom pays to sell ill-favored stock to the market. Do not give any feed to the turkeys for twelve hours before killing. This allows their crops and entrails to become empty and avoids much of the danger of spoiling. Full crops and entrails count against the value; they often taint the meat, and prevent it from being kept for any length of time.

DRESSING

Dry picking is always to be preferred when preparing fowl for market. When in fine condition, nicely picked, and sent to market without having been packed in ice, the turkey is at **its** best and consequently commands the highest price. When the fowl is plucked, hang its head down in a cool place until all the animal heat is gone from the body, being careful not to hang it where it will be exposed to the cold as it is likely to freeze. Do not **re-**move the head, feet or entrails, but have the whole carcass, including the head **and** feet, perfectly clean.

SHIPPING

For shipping, pack as closely as **pos-**sible into close boxes or barrels, nicely lined with white or manila paper. Do not use brown, soiled or printed paper. Have the package completely filled so as to prevent the poultry from shifting. Have all the heads laid one way, breasts up. Do not use hay or straw **for** packing as it marks and stains the fowl, detracting from the value. The above method can only be used when the poultry is sent to market without being packed in ice, and when this can be done in safety either in refrigerator cars or for a short distance in cold weather, it is by far the best.

The greater part, however, must be packed in ice. When necessary to do this, use nice clean barrels, cover the bottom with broken ice, then put in a layer of turkey, then a layer of ice; continue this until the barrel is packed full. Always use perfectly clean ice for packing. Head the barrel tightly, and mark its contents plainly on the head. Never ship mixed lots of poultry in the same package if it can be avoided.